YOU CAN

Senior Authors
Carl B. Smith
Virginia A. Arnold

Linguistics Consultant
Ronald Wardhaugh

Macmillan Publishing Co., Inc.
New York
Collier Macmillan Publishers
London

ACKNOWLEDGMENTS

The publisher gratefully acknowledges permission to reprint the following copyrighted material:

"Reading" from *Rhymes About Us* by Marchette Chute. Copyright © 1974 by Marchette Chute. Reprinted by permission of the publisher, E. P. Dutton, Inc.

"Sometimes" from *I Feel the Same Way* by Lilian Moore. Copyright © 1967 by Lilian Moore. (New York: Atheneum, 1967) Reprinted with the permission of Atheneum Publishers.

Illustrations: Ray Cruz, pp. 2-3; Loretta Lustig, pp. 4-9; Doreen Gay-Kassel, pp. 10-11; Olivia Cole, pp. 12-19; Lulu Delacre, pp. 20-27; Bill Ogden, pp. 28-35; Olivia Cole, pp. 36-37; Les Grey, pp. 38-43; Jan Pyk, pp. 54-61; Olivia Cole, pp. 62-63. **Photographs:** Robin Forbes, pp. 44-45; George Ancona, pp. 46-53. **Cover Design:** Jan Pyk.

Macmillan Publishing Co., Inc.
866 Third Avenue, New York, New York 10022
Collier Macmillan Canada, Inc.

Printed in the United States of America
ISBN 0-02-131660-0
9

Contents

You Can, *a story by Bette Davidson Kalash* 4

Reading, *a poem by Marchette Chute* 10

I Ride, *a story by Peter Martin Wortmann* 12

Jump Up, Jump Down,
a story by Judith Davis 20

Who Rides? *a story by Judith Davis* 28

SKILLS: Beginning Sounds 36

Big Dog, Little Dog,
a story by Harriet Ziefert 38

Sometimes, *a poem by Lilian Moore* 44

The Park, *a photo-essay by Bette Davidson Kalash* . . . 46

Nan, *a fantasy by Peter Martin Wortmann* 54

SKILLS: Vowel Sounds 62

Word List 64

YOU CAN

Bette Davidson Kalash

The man can fish.

Can you fish?

6

Now you can fish.

Boys and girls can jump.

Can you jump?

Now you can jump.

READING

A story is a special thing.

The ones that I have read,

They do not stay inside the books.

They stay inside my head.

—Marchette Chute

11

I Ride

Peter Martin Wortmann

He can see and ride.

I can ride.

He can see and ride.
Now I can see, too.

I see a man.

He rides.

The girls ride.

The boys ride, too.

17

Can I ride down?

I can.

I ride.

I see, too.

Now I can ride and see.

JUMP UP, JUMP DOWN

Judith Davis

Can I go to that house?

You can go to that house.

Jump up.

I like that house.

You can go, too.

Jump up.

Can he and I ride, too?

I like to see the fish.

Jump up.

I like that park.
Can I go, too?

You can go, but can't you see?
You can't go now.

I can go now.

I can ride to that park.

But I can't jump up.

I can't jump up.
I can jump down.

You can ride to the park.

Who Rides?

Judith Davis

29

Who rides?

Who rides up to the house?

Nan rides.

Jump down, Nan.

Go in.

Go in and sit down.

I can't see.

I can't see.

Sit down, girls and boys.

Sit down and you can see.

I like that, Nan.

Can I ride now?

I can't ride in the house.

33

You can go out.

You can go out and ride.

Who rides now?

Who can go out and ride?

I can.

I can.

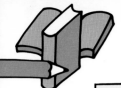

Beginning Sounds

 Hear	Read	Write
	jump girls	_girls_

man   ride   1. _____

he   boys   2. _____

house   but   3. _____

go   he   4. _____

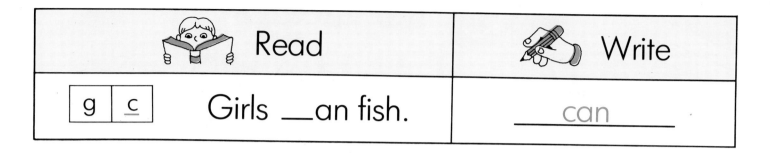 Read	Write
g | c Girls __an fish.	__can__

| r \| m | 1. Boys __ide to the park. |

| t \| g | 2. Girls go, __oo. |

| h \| m | 3. The girls see a __an. |

| t \| j | 4. He can __ump. |

| b \| r | 5. The __oys like to jump, too. |

Big Dog, Little Dog

Harriet Ziefert

The girls go into the park.
The dogs go into the park.

The girls jump up and down.

The big dog jumps.

The little dog jumps and jumps.

Down, big dog.
Down, little dog.
I like you, but sit down.

Go out of the park, big dog.
Go out of the park, little dog.

The dogs go out of the park.
The girls go out, too.

The dogs go into the house.
The big dog can sit in the house.
The little dog can, too.
Now the girls can jump.

Sometimes

Sometimes
when I skip or hop
or when I'm
    jumping

Suddenly
I like to stop
and listen to me
    thumping.

—Lilian Moore

THE PARK

Bette Davidson Kalash

Boys and girls like the park.

The big dog jumps.

Why does the dog jump up?

Why does that dog sit?

Can the dog see?

NO DOGS

Why can't the dog go in?
Can the dog read?

The dog can't read.
Boys and girls can read.

Why does the boy sit?
The boy can't ride.

Now the boy can ride.

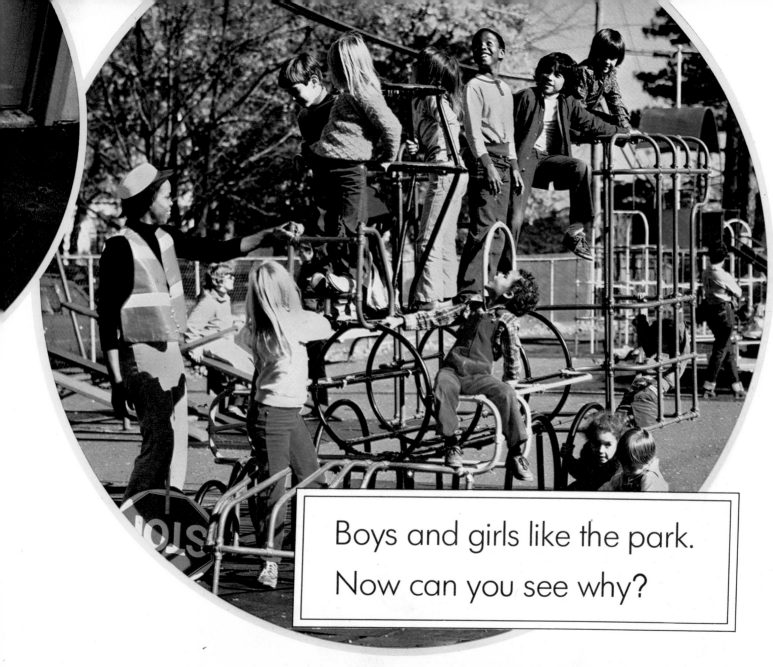

Boys and girls like the park.
Now can you see why?

Nan

Peter Martin Wortmann

The girl calls and calls.

Why does the girl call?

The girl calls one word.

The word is <u>Nan</u>.

Who is Nan?

Nan is a fish.

The girl calls a fish.

Why does the girl call a fish?

Why does the girl call Nan?

The girl likes to ride.

The girl likes to ride one fish.

The girl likes to ride and ride.

The girl calls to Nan.

The girl calls one word to Nan.

Now the word is <u>jump</u>.

The girl likes to ride.

Nan likes to jump.

Nan and the girl like to jump and jump.

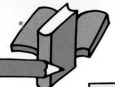

Vowel Sounds

Hear	Read	Write
	fish m<u>a</u>n	___man___

   now   Nan   1. _____

   can   big   2. _____

   dog   can't   3. _____

   sit   that   4. _____

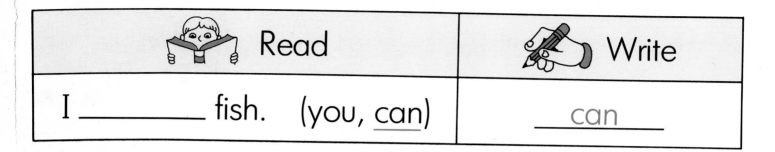

Read	Write
I _____ fish. (you, <u>can</u>)	*can*

1. The _____ likes to fish. (man, jump)

2. _____ likes to fish, too. (The, Nan)

3. The fish _____ see Nan. (boys, can't)

4. The man _____ see the fish. (can, sit)

5. Now Nan can see _____ fish. (dog, that)

WORD LIST

12. I	25. but	34. out	does
14. he	can't	38. big	50. read
15. too	28. who	dog	55. call
22. go	30. Nan	little	56. one
that	31. in	42. of	word
house	sit	48. why	is

To the Teacher: The words listed beside the page numbers above are instructional-vocabulary words introduced in *You Can.*

12. ride	dogs	52. boy	calls
39. into	40. jumps	55. girl	59. likes

To the Teacher: The children should be able to independently identify the applied-skills words listed beside the page numbers above by using previously taught phonics skills or by recognizing derived forms of words previously introduced.